AMAZING WONDERS

COLOSSEUM

BY LISA M. BOLT SIMONS

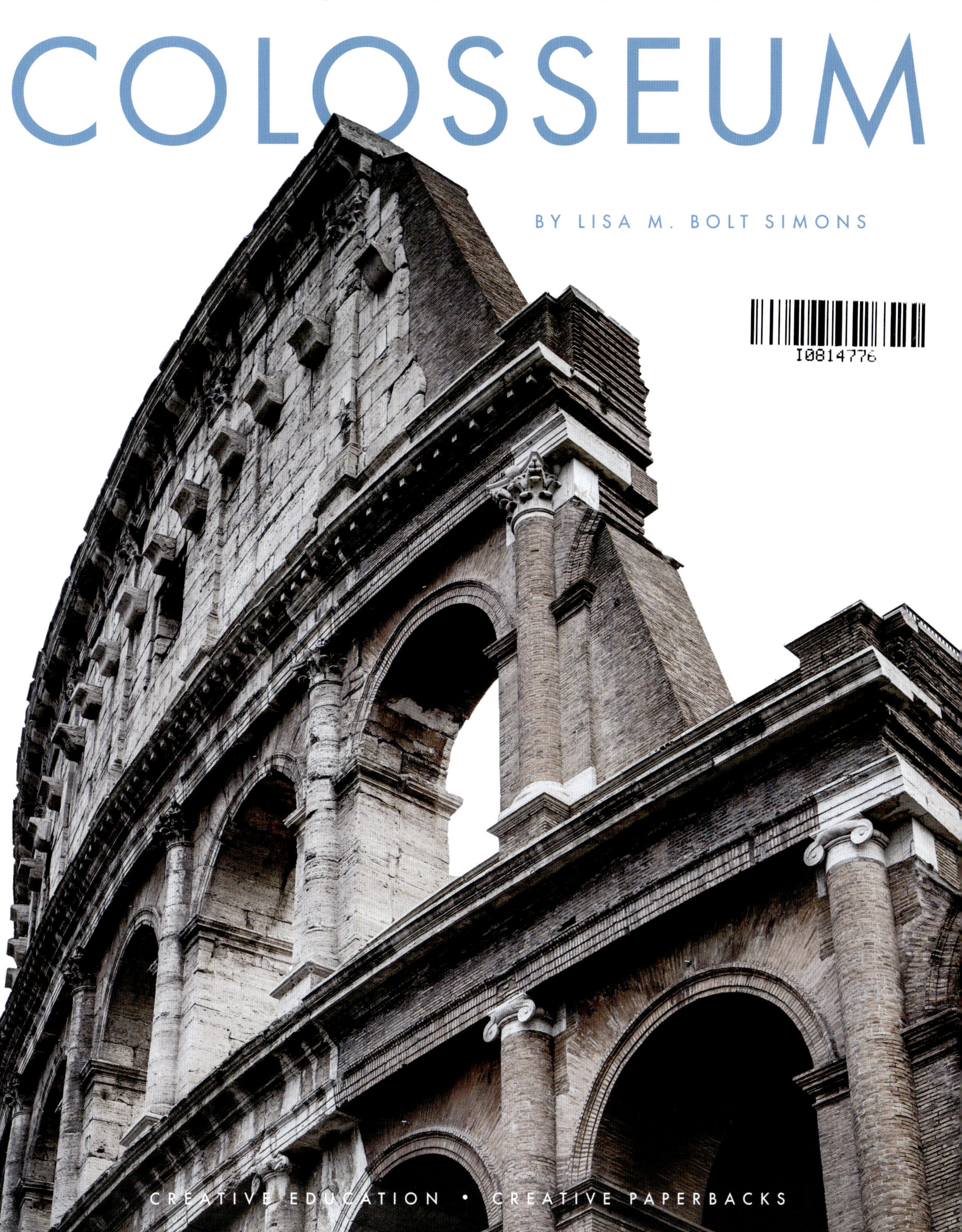

I0814776

CREATIVE EDUCATION • CREATIVE PAPERBACKS

Published by Creative Education and Creative Paperbacks
P.O. Box 227, Mankato, Minnesota 56002
Creative Education and Creative Paperbacks
are imprints of The Creative Company
www.thecreativecompany.us

Design by The Design Lab
Art direction by Graham Morgan
Edited by Jill Kalz

Images by Getty (mikroman6), iStock (DenPotisev), Pexels (Andrea Albanese, Chait Goli, Jason Renfrow Photography, Mark Neal), Unsplash (Federico Di Dio photography, Mathew Schwartz, Ruben Ramirez, Spencer Davis, Ümit Yıldırım), Wikimedia Commons (Kasa Fue)

Library of Congress Cataloging-in-Publication Data
Names: Simons, Lisa M. Bolt, 1969– author.
Title: Colosseum / Lisa M. Bolt Simons.
Description: Mankato, MN : Creative Education, Creative Paperbacks, [2025] Series: Amazing wonders | Includes bibliographical references and index. | Audience: Ages 6–9 | Audience: Grades 2–3 | Summary: "An elementary-level introduction to the ancient amphitheater in Rome, Italy, called the Colosseum, covering how, when, and why the Romans built the famous wonder. Includes captions, on-page definitions, additional resources, and an index"— Provided by publisher.
Identifiers: LCCN 2023042446 (print) | LCCN 2023042447 (ebook) | ISBN 9781640268579 (library binding) | ISBN 9781682774076 (paperback) | ISBN 9798889890195 (ebook)
Subjects: LCSH: Colosseum (Rome, Italy)—Juvenile literature. | Amphitheaters—Rome—Juvenile literature. | Rome (Italy)—Buildings, structures, etc.—Juvenile literature.
Classification: LCC DG68.1 .S56 2025 (print) | LCC DG68.1 (ebook) | DDC 937/.63—dc23/eng/20231113
LC record available at https://lccn.loc.gov/2023042446
LC ebook record available at https://lccn.loc.gov/2023042447

Printed in China

Table of Contents

Close to seven million people visit the Colosseum each year.

The Colosseum

(kah-luh-SEE-uhm) is a large **amphitheater**. It is nearly 2,000 years old. The building is famous for **gladiator** battles and fights between men and animals. It was later used as a church and then a castle.

amphitheater an oval or circular building with seats used for events

gladiator a trained fighter in ancient Rome

The Colosseum

is in west-central Italy. It stands in the city of Rome. Rome is Italy's capital. The Colosseum is in the center of the city.

The Colosseum could seat between 50,000 and 80,000 people.

Planning for the Colosseum began in the year 70. Construction lasted about 10 years. People celebrated the finished building with 100 days of games. They held gladiator battles and animal fights.

In the Colosseum, men fought each other for sport, sometimes to the death.

The Colosseum

was the idea of the Roman ruler at the time. Emperor Vespasian wanted the building to be a gift to the Roman people. He died before it was completed. His sons Titus and Domitian finished it in his name.

Vespasian ruled Rome for 10 years, from 69 to 79.

Vespasian had another reason to build the Colosseum. The ruler before him, Emperor Nero, had done many horrible things. Vespasian wanted to be remembered as a good man. He had the Colosseum built on Nero's former land.

The Colosseum was called the Flavian Amphitheater, after Flavian rulers Vespasian and his sons.

Builders used strong, natural stone called travertine for the outer walls.

Thousands of **enslaved** people built the Colosseum. They built vaults, or ceilings with arches. These vaults were made with heavy stone and concrete. Iron clamps held the stones together.

enslaved forced to work without pay or freedom

The Colosseum had four levels. Three levels had arches.

The Colosseum

had 76 arches to enter the building. The emperor used a private tunnel. There were two other special entrances. One was for gladiators. The other one was used to take out those who died in the arena.

arena the level area surrounded by seats on which events are held

The arena floor was removed in the 1800s.

When the Colosseum was built, the arena could be flooded. People brought in boats for pretend battles. Builders soon added tunnels underground called the hypogeum. Because of it, the arena above could no longer be flooded.

hypogeum an underground system of tunnels and rooms in the Colosseum

The Colosseum is an image of ancient Italy. It teaches us about the lives of people long ago. Much of the wonder has stood for nearly 2,000 years. It is one of the most visited places in the country.

The Colosseum has stood through wars, weather, and earthquakes.

Wonder Spotlight: Hidden Tunnels

The hypogeum was the underground part of the Colosseum. It had many rooms and tunnels. Gladiators and animals stayed there before they went into the arena. Eighty up-and-down passageways connected to the arena. Some of them had moving platforms. They moved larger animals, such as elephants and hippos. Some of the tunnels led outside the Colosseum. The area was restored and opened to the public in 2021.

Read More

Hansen, Grace. *Colosseum.* Minneapolis: Abdo Kids, 2018.

Jopp, Kelsey. *Colosseum.* Lake Elmo, Minn: Focus Readers, 2023.

Spanier, Kristine. *Colosseum.* Minneapolis: Jump!, 2021.

Websites

History: Colosseum
https://www.history.com/topics/ancient-rome/colosseum
Learn about the games held at the Colosseum.

National Geographic Kids: Ancient Rome
https://kids.nationalgeographic.com/history/article/ancient-rome
Read about the history of this powerful city.

Note: Every effort has been made to ensure that the websites listed above are suitable for children, that they have educational value, and that they contain no inappropriate material. However, because of the nature of the Internet, it is impossible to guarantee that these sites will remain active indefinitely or that their contents will not be altered.

Index